the little book of
LOVE SPELLS

First published in 2024 by OH
An Imprint of HEADLINE PUBLISHING GROUP

2 4 6 8 10 9 7 5 3 1

Disclaimer:

This book is intended for general informational purposes only and should not be relied upon as recommending or promoting any specific practice, diet or method of treatment. It is not intended to diagnose, advise, treat or prevent any illness or condition and is not a substitute for advice from a professional practitioner of the subject matter contained in this book. You should not use the information in this book as a substitute for medication, nutritional, diet, spiritual or other treatment that is prescribed by your practitioner. Furthermore, the publisher is not affiliated with and does not sponsor or endorse any uses of or beliefs about in any way referred in this book..

Cataloguing in Publication Data is available from the British Library

ISBN 978-1-80069-630-3

Compiled and written by: Katalin Németh
Editorial: Victoria Denne
Designed and typeset in Joanna Sans Nova by: Andy Jones
Project manager: Russell Porter
Illustrations: Freepik.com
Production: Arlene Lestrade
Printed and bound in China

Headline's policy is to use papers that are natural, renewable and recyclable products and made from wood grown in well-managed forests and other controlled sources. The logging and manufacturing processes are expected to conform to the environmental regulations of the country of origin.

HEADLINE PUBLISHING GROUP
An Hachette UK Company
Carmelite House, 50 Victoria Embankment, London EC4Y 0DZ

www.headline.co.uk   www.hachette.co.uk

the little book of
LOVE SPELLS

katalin németh

CONTENTS

Trigger warning:
This book explores themes that some
readers may find sensitive or distressing,
such as instances of violence, abuse, and
sexual assault.

Reader discretion is advised. Please take
care of yourself while reading.

INTRODUCTION

Love is one of the most powerful emotions. It can help us overcome impossible difficulties, cross the seven seas, and climb the highest mountains for the ones we love.

Love can show us heaven on earth and help us reach divinity through its boundless energy.

Love spells have been around since the dawn of time. Every culture has its own methods of bringing love into people's lives.

It's natural to want love, to want to be loved, and to want to protect that love.

Though love can allow us to reach new highs, it can also lead us to the deepest lows. We must be extremely self-aware when casting love spells, to ensure that we are practising them with the best intentions.

In this book we will discuss all kinds of love spells, except one: how to force someone to "fall in love" with you. This particular spell can bring unwanted consequences for both you and the other person or people involved.

Let's think about it. You meet someone, they are good-looking, funny, and have certain qualities that you are looking for. You fall head over heels for them, but for some reason, they don't like you back. You put a love spell on them, and it works!

In the first few days, you are ecstatic. But then it becomes apparent that the love your crush feels is superficial. You will forever question whether their feelings are real, making it difficult to foster trust and intimacy.

You might discover that you don't like this person after all, but the spell binds them to you, and your relationship could become toxic, obsessive, or abusive. You could, of course, break the spell, but why go to all this trouble? And what if you missed your chance to meet your true love in the meantime?

The internet is full of "sure-fire love spells" to force someone into loving you. But before trying them out, consider how you would feel if a person forced you to love them against your will.

Instead, this book contains spells to bring you a lover who serves your best interest and loves and cherishes you for who you are. You will find spells to protect your relationship, strengthen bonds, banish outside influences, and help you love yourself. When you are happy inside, you are ready and able to share that happiness with others. When you truly love and accept yourself, it will be easier to find your tribe.

I wish you wisdom and joy for your journey. Blessed be!

CHAPTER

1

WHERE TO START?

There should be ample planning going into spellcasting. You want to make sure the spell works, and that it works the way you intended it.

Depending on how complicated a spell is, you may wish to consider the day of the week, the Moon's phase, or even the zodiac sign the Moon is currently in.

You may also want to add extra power to your spell by including accessories, such as an altar, food, or a talisman.

The opportunities are endless. Anything and everything can become part of your practice. The Queen of Hearts from a deck of poker cards can become a magical representation of you, or even a barbie doll or your favourite mug. Sympathetic magic works by acting out the results you want to see in real life.

How you do this is entirely up to you – they only need to be meaningful to you. The spells in this book are good to use, but you can always customize them as you like.

Before performing any kind of magic, the first steps are always cleansing, grounding, and protection.

Only when these are in place should you attempt spellcasting, especially bigger spells that require a lot of focus.

Not only do these steps help you focus your intention, they protect you from negative forces, too.

CLEANSING

To start your ritual, first cleanse yourself and your spellcasting space. It could be a quick sweeping of the floor, followed by a thorough hand wash. It could also be a ritual bath with oils and herbs and a deep cleaning of the whole house. Adjust the intensity according to your needs.

After cleansing your physical surroundings, take care of the energies in your space.

Smudging is a popular way of spiritual cleansing. Use bunches of white sage, bay leaves, rosemary, or, if you feel extreme negativity, dry red chillies.

Light your herbs, and when they start to smoke, walk around your space, making sure the smoke spreads everywhere.

It is a good idea to open the windows beforehand, to allow the smoke and negative energies to escape.

If you can't use smoke, sprinkle blessed water around your spellcasting space. Homemade salt water or Moon water are both excellent for this purpose, as is holy water.

GROUNDING

Sit in your spellcasting space and settle your mind. Ground yourself in the present; let all other worries take their place in the back of your mind, shelved away for later. Concentrate on the spell you are going to perform. Run through its steps in your mind, and make sure you have everything you need ready for it.

Close your eyes and imagine a beam
of energy connecting you to the
centre of the earth. All your worries,
all your woes leave you through it, and
are being burned in the magma's
extreme heat.

In their place, you are filled with radiant
energy from the very core of the planet.
Energy that can move continents.

Now visualize a bubble of dazzling light surrounding you and filling up the whole casting space. It keeps away negative energies and invites helping entities into the space.

Visualization is an important skill to practise – some of the most powerful spells can be achieved purely through visualization.

Ask your spirit guides, or any spirit you are working with, to enter this space and aid you in your work.

Cast a magic circle. This could be a visible line drawn with salt or an energy circle invisible to the eye. Cast it clockwise, and make sure all your ingredients are included inside it.

You are now ready to cast your spell.

PLANNING a SPELL

Just like causing the ebb and flow of the tides, the Moon influences the type of energies you can tap into when casting your spell.

the PHASES of the MOON

There are four main phases of the Moon's cycle, and each phase has its own distinctive energy you can utilize.

the NEW MOON

The New Moon is for letting go of what doesn't serve you, banishing spells, and self-care.

the WAXING MOON

The Waxing Moon is for new beginnings and nurturing relationships.

the FULL MOON

The Full Moon is for manifestation, gratitude, and celebration.

the WANING MOON

The Waning Moon is for rest, forgiveness, sharing, and charity.

the MOON
in different ZODIAC SIGNS

To further strengthen your spell's power, you could consider timing it when the Moon enters the different Zodiac signs.

Moon in Aries is best for new beginnings and self-confidence.

Moon in Taurus is best to deal with money and property, abundance, and sensual pleasures.

Moon in Gemini is best for communication, creative writing, and technology.

Moon in Cancer is best focused on family life, fertility, healing, and forgiveness.

Moon in Leo is suited for networking, building rapport, performing for others, and confidence.

Moon in Virgo is best for service, healing, and selflessness.

Moon in Libra is the time for mediation, diplomacy, arts, and studies.

Moon in Scorpio is well suited for spicing up your sex life, strengthening allegiances, and for unveiling secrets.

Moon in Sagittarius is great for travel, re-examining your beliefs and ethics, excitement, and novelty.

Moon in Capricorn is the best time for business matters, perseverance, and discipline.

Moon in Aquarius is good for creative projects and reinventing yourself.

Moon in Pisces is the time for spirituality, shadow work, and magic.

the DAYS of the WEEK

Monday is the day of the Moon, and so it is connected with the sacred feminine, intuition, dreamwork, and emotions. It is a good day for divination and healing.

Tuesday is associated with Tyr, Norse god of war. It is a good day for action and defence, and for getting things done.

Wednesday is associated with Odin, Norse god of magic and the runes. It is a good day for communication and intellectual projects.

Thursday is associated with Thor, Norse god of power and protection. It is a good day for seeking justice and protection and taking your power back.

Friday is associated with Freyja, Norse goddess of love, fertility, war, and the dead. It is the best day for any type of love magic.

Saturday is associated with Loki and Saturn, Norse and Roman gods of mischief, planning, and karma. It is a good day for banishing spells and finding out and facing the truth.

Sunday is associated with the Sun, and so it is connected with the sacred masculine, health, wealth, and prosperity. It is a good day for spells to bring a bit of fun in the relationship, for healing, and for growing what is already there.

CHAKRAS

Chakras are energy centres in the body that sit along the spine. They are associated with different functions and areas of life. If one is blocked, it will cause difficulties in the flow of energy in the whole body, and it will affect your quality of life.

When doing manifestation, shadow work, or setting up an altar, use this list of the chakras and associated attributes to ease your manifestation and healing.

For example, if you are setting up an altar to unblock your heart chakra after a difficult breakup, you will want to fill your sacred space with green and pink colours, and wear clothes matching this palette.

There are also smells, internal organs, yoga poses, and exercises associated with the chakras.

the seven main chakras

The chakra energy points start at the root, or base, of the spine and extend to the crown of the head. Opening up these chakras from root to crown reflects the journey of spiritual ascent.

1 **the root chakra**
2 **the sacral chakra**
3 **the solar plexus chakra**
4 **the heart chakra**
5 **the throat chakra**
6 **the third eye chakra**
7 **the crown chakra**

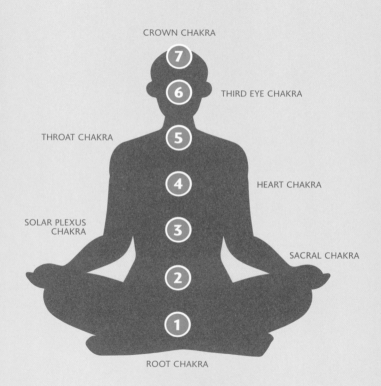

CROWN CHAKRA

THIRD EYE CHAKRA

THROAT CHAKRA

HEART CHAKRA

SOLAR PLEXUS
CHAKRA

SACRAL CHAKRA

ROOT CHAKRA

Root Chakra (red and black) – the seat of action, passion, and lust.

Sacral Chakra (orange) – the seat of playfulness, spontaneity, teamwork, and exploration.

Solar Plexus Chakra (yellow) – the seat of self-esteem, inspiration, and empowerment.

Heart Chakra (green and pink) – the seat of giving and receiving love.

Throat Chakra (turquoise) – the seat of communication and self-expression.

Third Eye Chakra (blue, indigo) – the seat of intuition, creativity, and magic.

Crown Chakra (purple and white) – the seat of spiritual advancement.

CRYSTALS

Crystals are amazing aids in witchcraft and energy work, and they are readily available almost anywhere in the world. People have been utilizing their healing and empowering properties for millennia, from ancient Egypt to native South America.

Take care when shopping for crystals as there are many fake ones in circulation. As a rule of thumb, if it is too cheap to be true, it usually isn't a real crystal and may instead be coloured glass.

Crystals are usually denser and heavier than fake stones, and if you are sensitive to it, you can actually feel their power.

Try to buy your crystals from a trusted, ethical seller.

The most common crystals used in witchcraft are the following:

ONYX

- for protection, cleansing, and grounding
- associated with the Root Chakra

  Stones with similar properties are jasper, hematite, bloodstone, and rhodonite.

TIGER'S EYE

- for motivation, clarity, and energy
- associated with the Sacral Chakra

  Stones with similar properties are goldstone, carnelian, and orange calcite.

CITRINE

- for focus, creativity, memory, joy, and strength
- associated with the Solar Plexus Chakra

  Stones with similar properties are amber, yellow jasper, and sunstone.

ROSE QUARTZ

- for self-love, love, and bliss
- associated with the Heart Chakra

  Stones with similar properties are unakite, emerald, aventurine, jade, and malachite.

LAPIS LAZULI

- for speaking your truth and justice
- associated with the Throat Chakra

  Stones with similar properties are turquoise, aquamarine, and amazonite.

AMATHYST

- for spirituality, protection, dreams, and intuition
- associated with the Third Eye Chakra

  Stones with similar properties are sodalite, labradorite, obsidian, and tourmaline.

CLEAR QUARTZ

- for clarity, self-esteem, trust, and focus
- associated with the Crown Chakra

  Stones with similar properties are selenite, howlite, and moonstone.

essential OILS and INCENSE

Smells can play an important role in witchcraft. The more of your senses you activate during spellcasting, the more focused, and therefore more successful, you will be. Incense sticks and cones are also a common type of offering to spirits.

Always listen to your body. If scents tend to hurt your head, leave them out of your practice.

The most commonly used fragrances are:

PATCHOULI

- for grounding and balance
- associated with the **Root Chakra**

  Other scents associated with this chakra are cedarwood and myrrh.

SANDALWOOD

- for spirituality, purity, and rituals
- associated with the **Sacral Chakra**

  Other scents associated with this chakra are jasmine and citruses.

BERGAMOT

- for joy, self-confidence, and assertiveness
- associated with the **Solar Plexus Chakra**

  Other scents associated with this chakra are vetiver and cinnamon.

ROSE

- for love, nurturing, gentleness, and calming
- associated with the **Heart Chakra**

  Other scents associated with this chakra are eucalyptus and marjoram.

CHAMOMILE

- for calmness, balance, and impartiality
- associated with the **Throat Chakra**

  Other scents associated with this chakra are myrrh, peppermint, and cypress.

HYACINTH

- for connection to loved ones and spirits
- associated with the **Third Eye Chakra**

  Other scents associated with this chakra are violet and geranium.

FRANKINCENSE

- for cleansing, higher self, and inner peace
- associated with the **Crown Chakra**

  Other scents associated with this chakra are lavender and rose tree.

Incense and scents that go well with any type of spell work include nag champa, sandalwood, and frankincense. If you are on a budget, one of these should last you a good few spells.

If you worry about the smoke alarm going off, open your windows before using incense sticks. Alternatively, use essential oils with a diffuser instead.

You can incorporate these scents into your daily life, too, in the form of shower gels and perfumes, to keep your focus on your spellwork.

KITCHEN WITCHERY

Incorporating herbs, spices, and other food items can be beneficial, especially with spells that aim to ground you in a situation.

Involving more senses increases the chance of success, and there is a special power in spells that you can consume.

Food items are also often offered to spirits, which is a nice thing to do if you are working with any kind of entity from the other side.

When selecting your ingredients for your spell, first identify which chakra it corresponds with. Then, simply choose fruits and vegetables of the colour the chakra is associated with.

For example, the Root Chakra is associated with red root vegetables, like carrots and beets. The Crown Chakra is associated with purple and white vegetables, like cauliflowers and aubergines. Be creative in your kitchen, and try to incorporate these ingredients in your cooking as often as possible.

Root Chakra: nettle, sage, dandelion, beetroot, carrot, ginger, turmeric.

Sacral Chakra: orange, hibiscus, cinnamon, clove, calendula, red berries, pumpkins.

Solar Plexus Chakra: lemon, fennel, lemongrass, peppermint, oats.

Heart Chakra: rose, marjoram, cilantro, saffron, green tea, green vegetables.

Throat Chakra: honey, black pepper, chamomile, thyme, dark berries, grapes.

Third Eye Chakra: lavender, tulsi, cardamom, rosemary, poppy seeds, chocolate.

Crown Chakra: ginseng, gingko, tulsi, lavender, cabbage, cauliflower.

Folk Magic often uses cooked or baked food items in spellcasting.

Putting your intention into your cooking will make a difference in your everyday life, too.

CHAPTER

2

SELF-LOVE

*Self-love
is not a new-age
trend but
a basic human
necessity for a
healthy life.*

The ancient Greeks recognized the importance of self-love and named it *philautia*, literally translating to, "the love of the self".

Without loving yourself and being comfortable with who you are, it can be hard to love others.

You can't pour from an empty cup.

Of course, it is possible to perform acts of love, but not without the risk of resentment, doubt, unmet expectations, and, eventually, burning out, or worse, being taken advantage of.

On the other hand, to find true love and friendships, you need to show your true self. And to do that you need to unapologetically love and accept yourself.

Many people end up in situations where they are unhappy or being taken advantage of because they weren't comfortable with expressing themselves, and therefore didn't find the people who could have loved them for who they are.

MAGICAL MOTIVATION

You need to put the work into loving yourself, too. Unfortunately, self-love doesn't always come naturally, but with focused work and intent, it is possible.

To address the areas you feel uncomfortable with, write a list of them, and figure out solutions. There might be things you cannot change, but there will be ones that you can.

You might write "I look drab in photos". As a solution, actively research what kind of clothes to wear that might suit you better, tailored for your skin tone, your body type, the situation, and so on. You could also find inspiration photos for poses, backgrounds, colours, and more.

You might write "I let others walk over me, I ignore the red flags". You will need to work on how you see yourself and build stronger boundaries.

Write a list of things you are not willing to compromise on for anyone and behaviours you wouldn't tolerate from anyone. Stick to these principles, no matter what, and walk away if they are ignored. You are better off alone than in a situation where you are being taken advantage of.

Writing down all these steps can be overwhelming. It is no wonder, then, that taking the first steps can be extremely daunting.

A talisman and an altar or vision board can make the process a lot easier.

how to CREATE a TALISMAN

Items you could use for creating a talisman are endless. It could be a crystal necklace – fluorite or clear quartz are perfect. It could be an essential oil diffuser – rosemary, douglas fir, or frankincense are great for focus. It could even be a completely normal keychain, a small charm, or even a toy.

Some people find it helpful to keep a small figurine or picture of their role model with them to increase their focus through the archetype. For example, action figures are great for keeping up a fitness regime.

To make a talisman, first you need to cleanse your item. Holding it under flowing water is the best way to do this, but be mindful of your item's material. If you think running water might damage it, wipe it with a wet cloth instead.

If you chose an object made of paper, like a photo or money, use the element of air instead of water, and blow away any residual energy that might be clinging to it.

After cleansing, hold the item to your heart, and infuse it with your energy.

Concentrate on your goal and on the archetype you need the item to represent.

Treat this item as a living being. Greet it when you see it, open up to it if you made a mistake – the more intimate connection you build with your talisman, the better it will work.

It is worth noting that you are not possessing it with any kind of spirit. Talismans work with your own energy; they are a psychological tool. They might develop a "personality", which is the result of the normal function of the human mind.

Just like different tarot decks can have different "personalities", your talisman could become compassionate, strict, or sassy, depending on your own qualities.

Take the talisman with you everywhere or keep it in one designated place where you can gain strength from its presence while performing your task.

It is a good idea to cleanse and recharge it from time to time. To do this, just repeat the whole process from the start with the same item, unless it needs replacing due to wear and tear.

how to build an
an ALTAR or
a VISION
BOARD

Identify which chakra's energy you will need to strengthen to make your task easier and set up your altar in its colours.

If it is love-related, dress your altar in pink and green, for the Heart Chakra.

If it is passion-related, dress it in red.

If it is something intellectual, use blues and yellows.

Decorate your altar with items you connect with, things that make you happy and that you associate with your goal. You don't need expensive things on your altar; an interesting feather or rock is just as good as a store-bought statue. Make it your own, and don't worry about what it "should" look like.

Spend some time every day looking at the altar, reminding yourself why you are doing this. The action of consciously directing your mind to think about your goal will aid your determination to see it through.

If you are religious, you could request the help of your god to achieve your goal. Keep an object on the altar that represents your god and make regular offerings.

Whenever you look at the altar, remember that you are strong. You've got this!

a spell for

ACCEPTING YOURSELF

Everyone has flaws; we are only humans. Making peace with this fact is the first step towards accepting yourself.

For this spell, you will need:
- A piece of paper
- A red pen
- A green pen

Fold the paper in half. With the red pen, write your flaws on the left side of the paper. Write down everything that bothers you about yourself. All your physical imperfections, all your personality traits that drive you mad.

When you're done with the list, sit with it for a few moments. Are these really such huge issues? Is there anything non-magical you can do to fix them?

Now take the green pen and rephrase your flaws on the right side of the paper. Think about it as a "what is your greatest weakness" question at a job interview.

You admitted you have these flaws, now you need to find ways to see them from a positive, constructive angle.

For example, if you wrote "I am too judgemental", you could change it to "My ancestors and I needed to be judgemental in order to survive in society, I acknowledge that.
But times are different. I am safe, and I am working on being more accepting, inclusive, and open-minded."

Or if you wrote "I hate the stretch marks on my thighs", you could change it to "My skin had to stretch in order to achieve what was needed – a pregnancy, a growth spurt, or a sudden weight gain for whatever reason. My skin helped me cope with this difficulty, and I came out victorious. My marks are battle scars; they are the stripes of a tiger, the marks of a fighter."

When you have rephrased everything on your list, tear the paper in half.

Take the half with the red writing, and tear it into small pieces. That mindset belongs to the past and is irrelevant in the present.

Flush the pieces down the toilet by closing the lid, and flushing three times to make sure all the pieces are gone before you open the lid again.

After washing your hands, take the half with the green writing and keep it in a personal place where you can see it and be reminded of it often. Under your pillow, in your purse, or on your fridge are all great places.

This is your new mindset. You are proud of who you are and no longer need to hide any part of yourself.

Implement your new mentality into practice by being mindful of how you talk about yourself and how you carry yourself in social situations. Keep your self-talk in check, learn to take compliments, and most importantly, believe them. Compliment others honestly, because uplifting others will lift your spirit.

Remember your quirks will be the little things someone will fall in love with.

Don't hide who you are.

a spell for **LETTING** your **QUIRKS LOOSE**

For this spell, you will need:
- A brightly coloured piece of paper and pen
- A white or yellow candle
- Bergamot or cinnamon essential oil
- A mirror

Your quirks make you who you are. They act like the beam of a lighthouse for kindred spirits to find you. Sometimes mistaken for imperfections, your quirks are what make you unique and different to others in a world where many strive to be the same.

Still, it can be daunting to be yourself in public. We are conditioned to conform to the norm, and of course there are situations when you need to tone yourself down. But when it is safe, never hesitate to express exactly who you are!

Set up the mirror on your altar. Light the candle and sit with your reflection for a few moments. Smile at yourself and acknowledge how uniquely beautiful you are.

Write down 22 things that you love about yourself on the piece of paper. 22 is a master number – it encompasses both spiritual and practical skills and lessons. Write down every little thing you like about yourself, especially if it is unconventional. You are kind, you are good at maths, you can crochet, you know how to train cats; everything counts.

Fold the list and keep it under the candle on your altar. It will remind you of how awesome you are when you are not on top of your game, so take care of it.

Now choose one of the most important things from your list. It has to be a thing that feeds your soul rather than your body. Whether it is your gender identity, your sexual orientation, your oldest hobby, or your favourite genre of music, it doesn't matter, there are no wrong answers.

Choose how you will display your love for this thing every day from now on.

It doesn't have to be big.

Buy a badge representing your chosen things, paint your nails the colour that represents it to you, or join an online club. It is entirely up to you how you do it – the main thing is that you keep your spark alive and show it to the world.

Anoint your reflection in the mirror with the bergamot oil, and say:

"I show the world my weird side,

I attract my own tribe.

Real friends are now coming to me,

So it is and so mote it be!"

Let the candle burn down completely and leave the list on your altar permanently. Incorporate bergamot into your daily life. Use it as a perfume to boost your radiant self-confidence.

Remember, only do this if you have a safe, supporting environment. If you think showing your true self could get you in trouble, consider waiting until you are in a better, safer space.

There will be a time when you can be who you really are, and maybe even advocate for others. But only when you are away from immediate harm.

CHAPTER
3

ROMANTIC
LOVE

DEITIES
and SPIRITS
of LOVE

Working with deities is one of
the best ways to ensure the success
of your spell.

Before petitioning any deity for help, always offer them something in exchange as a show of respect and appreciation.

Building a lasting relationship with spirits can supercharge not only your love spells, but also your entire practice going forward.

a LIST of SPIRITS and DEITIES of LOVE from AROUND the WORLD

Archangel Raphael is the angel of healing. This includes healing a broken heart. Many people ask him for guidance to find their perfect spouse, too. Offer him green candles and anything associated with healing.

Aphrodite/Venus is the Greek/Roman goddess of love, beauty, and lust. She can be of help with love spells and sex-related magic. Offer her roses, perfume, or pearls.

St Valentine is the patron saint of love, best known for Valentine's Day. Many ask him for guidance in marriage or before making things official, to ensure a long-lasting relationship. Offer him red or pink candles and food items associated with love. Fasting is another way to show your dedication.

Kama is the Hindu god of lust. Offer him flowers, sweets, or fruits.

St Agnes is the patron saint of purity, engaged couples, and survivors of abuse. Offer her white candles, silver coins, or woollen clothing.

Freyja is the Norse goddess of love, fertility, war, and the dead. She represents both the radiance and the dark side of femininity and can be petitioned for help with manifesting or banishing a lover. Offer her mead, apples, honey, or jewellery.

Aine is the Irish goddess of love, summer, and wealth. Offer her summer fruits and berries, eggs, or gold.

Bastet is the feline-headed Egyptian goddess of love and fertility. Offer her alcohol or meat.

Ishtar is the Sumerian goddess of love and fertility. Offer her any home-cooked food, especially fish, meat, and grains.

Eros is the Greek god of lust. Offer him rose and jasmine flowers or pink or red candles.

Shiva is the Hindu god of destruction, but he is also considered to be an ideal husband, and many women petition him to help them find their perfect spouse. Offer him milk, honey, yoghurt, fruits or sweets. If you can get hold of it, he loves bel fruits and leaves.

LGBTQ+

-friendly deities

In modern India, the LGBTQ+ community often worships and identifies with gender-diverse deities.

Forms of **Shiva** and **Shakti** can be worshipped as non-binary deities, particularly the Ardhanarishvara form.

Vishnu is another non-binary Hindu deity, whose female form, **Mohini,** has a prominent role in Hindu sagas.

Harihara, the united form of **Shiva** and Vishnu, is also a popular choice.

Offer these deities candles, vegetarian food, water, flowers, or sweets.

St Sebastian, a Christian saint and martyr, is also worth mentioning as a long-standing queer icon.

The symbolism of his almost completely naked body pierced by arrows has long resonated with the gay community. Offer him flowers, candles, or food.

In ancient Greece, **Zeus**, **Apollo**, **Hermes**, **Achilles**, and even **Heracles** have myths tying them to the LGBTQ+ community.

Love between two men was widely accepted in ancient Greece, and everyone has heard of the enormously talented Sappho, the lesbian poetess, who wrote her heart-wrenchingly beautiful poetry about women.

Feel free to do more research and choose a deity you resonate with.

In Norse myths, the most well-known god to have changed gender and engaged in procreation in their changed form is **Loki**, who not only mothered the eight-legged horse Sleipnir, but all the witches of the world, too.

The modern pagan community considers him/them, along with **Frey**, a perfect patron for the genderqueer and LGBTQ+ community.

Offer Loki sweet or spicy food, handmade items – especially shiny things, or alcohol.

Offer Frey honey, mead, meat, food grains, or gold.

the WHEEL of the YEAR

The Wheel of the Year represents
the annual cycle of seasonal festivals
or celebrations, marking the Earth's
journey through the solar year.

It is typically divided into eight major
festivals, often celebrated through
rituals and ceremonies that align with
the changing seasons and natural cycles.

a spell to MEET your TRUE LOVE

For this spell you will need:
- Rice pudding prepared with your own hands
- The Waxing Gibbous Moon on a clear Friday night

This spell aims to ensure you meet your true love before the next festival on the **Wheel of the Year**. You will not know what they are called or what they look like, but you will feel it in your heart when you meet them.

Give the spell at least two weeks to work. If the next festival is sooner than that, then aim for the one after that. For example, if Samhain is just a week away, ask the Moon to bring your lover by Yule.

Before performing your ritual, make sure you are ready to go to sleep directly afterwards. Brush your teeth, put on your pyjamas, and complete all tasks beforehand, or the spell could be broken.

Cook your rice pudding in the evening, concentrating on the spell. Rice, milk, and sugar are symbolic of love, nurturing, and fertility.

Mix three spoons of rose water in your pudding while cooking to give it an extra magical kick. The fragrance of rose water will please the Moon and help lead your lover to you.

Do not taste the pudding before the ritual is done. Be especially careful not to burn it, and if you do, discard the whole thing and start over.

Serve the pudding on your ritual plate.

When the Moon is high up in the sky, go outside, and raise your plate in her direction. Offer the pudding to her and ask her to lead your true love – who serves your higher self and purpose – to you before the next festival. Then say:

"For you, Mother Moon, this gift I bring.

Like true love, it is fragrant and sweet.

Bring my true love before Yule to me,

So it is and so mote it be!"

Eat three spoons of the pudding and leave the rest outside for the night. Without doing anything else, go to sleep, knowing that you will dream about your true love.

Don't worry if you don't remember the dream the next morning. It will be stored in your subconscious, and you will feel the connection when the time comes.

a spell to

MANIFEST

your # PERFECT

LOVER

For this spell you will need:
- A piece of paper and a pen
- A sweet potato

On your paper, write down all the personality traits that you'd like your next partner to have. You can be as detailed as you like or you could just write "they should be right for my higher self and purpose". Fold it up as small as possible, so it fits into the potato.

Cook or bake the sweet potato without any seasoning. Cut it in half and place your list between the two halves. Put it back together and go out into nature with it.

In a secluded spot, sit down, draw a magic circle around you, and focus on your intention.

Petition the Universe to send this person into your life. Meditate and visualize them, and call out to them, letting them know you are waiting for them.

Don't doubt they have heard you, and they are on their way. It is only a matter of time.

Place the sweet potato on the ground,
offering it to Mother Earth, who will
carry your call to your lover.

Undo the magic circle and leave
the sweet potato behind for wildlife to
consume it.

a spell to CHOOSE from SUITORS

If you have more than one person interested in you, or you have a crush on more than one, this is a spell that can help you decide.

For this spell you will need:
- All-purpose flour
- A piece of paper and a pen
- Water

Cut your paper into small strips and write the names of your suitors on them.

Make a thick, firm dough with the flour and water. It should be a little harder than playdough.

Divide the dough into balls big enough to hide a paper strip.

Fold up your paper strips and hide them in the balls of dough.

Use as many balls as required for the number of suitors you have, and that many again for blank paper strips.
So, if you have two suitors, you should make four balls.

Make sure all balls are equally heavy.

Heat plenty of water in a saucepan, and when it is boiling, place the balls into it, all at the same time.

Whichever ball comes up to the surface first, that is the best choice for you at this point in time. If you get a blank strip of paper, you might want to consider rejecting all your suitors, at least for now.

a spell to **KEEP PROBLEMS at BAY**

For this spell you will need:
- 9 bay leaves
- The Waning Moon on a Tuesday or Thursday

To protect your existing relationship from external stressors, perform this spell with the consent of your partner.

Take a shower and ask your partner to do the same. Wear fresh, clean clothes, and perform this spell either in your living room or your bedroom.

Draw a magic circle around you and your partner. If you have a friend you can trust, ask them to light the bunch of bay leaves and walk around the two of you, gently wafting the smoke of the leaves towards you.

Draw a magic circle around you and your partner. If you have a friend you can trust, ask them to light the bunch of bay leaves and walk around the two of you, gently wafting the smoke of the leaves towards you.

If you are doing the spell alone, wave the bunch above your heads in circles. Then say together:

"Outside forces stay away,

Jealous vipers kept at bay,

They can't divide you and me,

So it is and so mote it be!"

Repeat the spell three times in unison.

Place the bay leaves on a fireproof dish and let them burn down. Hug your partner and undo the magic circle.

Strengthen the spell by spending quality time together, playing, cooking, or in bed.

the MAGIC
of MAY DAY
DEW

Just before dawn on May 1, go outside to your garden or a park.

When the sun rises, bathe yourself in the dew on the grass and flowers that surround you.

Cover as much of your skin with it as possible. This will make you as radiant as the dew drops reflecting the first rays of sunshine and allow many potential suitors to discover your inner beauty in the coming year.

CHAPTER

4

BROKEN
HEART

a spell for
FORGIVENESS

For this spell you will need:

- A piece of paper and a red pen
- Red thread
- Two feathers from the same type of bird
- A cauldron or fireproof dish
- Bay leaves, sage, and lavender – one piece or cutting from each
- Wood shavings or kindling
- The New Moon, preferably on Saturday

Forgiving those who have hurt you
releases your heart from the clutches
of anger and resentment and frees
up that energy to be used for moving
on and being able to love again.

Know that you can forgive someone
without letting them back into
your life.

Write down everything that the person you want to forgive has done to you. Make it as long as it has to be. Be as vulgar or sarcastic as you like; no one will ever read it. Pour all your anger and hurt into it.

When it is done, roll or fold up the paper, and tie it with the red thread. Tie one of the feathers to it, for it to carry the contents away.

Start a fire in the cauldron. Add the
herbs. When the flames are strong
enough, light the list you wrote, and
let it burn. Let the flames consume
your anger and release it with the
smoke that rises from it.

Go outside and release the ashes into
the wind, far from your home. When
you arrive home, place the remaining
feather onto your altar. If you ever feel
resentment in your heart, it will remind
you that it is over now. It might take
time, but you will get there.

a spell to # HEAL a BROKEN HEART

For this spell you will need:
- Two white roses
- Bird seeds
- An open space with birdsong
- The Full or Waning Moon on Monday

Heartbreak is one of the most painful things you can experience. This spell is aimed at easing that pain and helping you let your lover go.

Go out into nature. This is the time to touch grass and listen to the sounds of the forest. If you don't have a forest nearby, a park should do it, as long as it has trees and birdsong and is relatively far from people and traffic.

Try to be there at sunrise or sunset, when the birds sing loudest.

Sit down under a tree and rest your head on its trunk. Take a few deep breaths and take time to enjoy your environment.

Fill your heart with this tranquillity. Cry if you are moved to. Express your sadness before starting the ritual.

When you are ready, place the two roses in front of you on the ground, and say:

"Birds of song, hear my plea,

Take this heartbreak away from me,

Fill my heart with peace and glee,

So it is and so mote it be!"

While chanting, draw a circle around your roses with the bird seeds. Be generous in your offering, because the task you're asking of the birds is heavy.

Sit with your roses for a while.

If a bird or any animal comes to eat the seeds while you are there, consider it an especially good omen.

Take one of the roses, thank the forest for its help, and go home.

Place the rose under your pillow and know that it will absorb all your sadness and grief while you sleep.

In the morning, go outside and bury the rose in the ground. You can do this in your garden, a pot of dirt, or in the park or forest you performed the ritual in.

a spell to BREAK a LOVE SPELL

For this spell you will need:

- A black candle
- A photo of you and your partner as a couple
- Something that belongs to to your partner
- Something that belongs to you
- A cauldron or a fireproof dish

When you are under a love spell, you can't stop thinking about the person, even when that person is abusive or has broken up with you already. You don't understand how you still can't let that person go, or why you are with them in the first place.

Not being able to let go of someone toxic can also happen because of a trauma bond, which we will discuss in the last chapter.

Never try to break a love spell on someone else unless you have informed consent. If you are not sure they are under a spell, try to confirm it first through a medium or through divination, and ask for permission before performing any rituals.

If you are the one who performed the love spell, you can simply undo it by modifying the original spell, reversing its actions.

The following spell is for the case of someone else having cast a spell on you.

If you don't have a photo, take a piece of paper. Draw a heart in the middle and write your names into it: your name on the left, your partner's name on the right. It should be easy to tear the heart in two and separate your names by doing so.

Light the candle and focus your will on breaking the love spell that you are under. Take the photo or the paper and tear it in half in a way that means you are separated completely. Then say three times:

"I break this spell you put on me,

So it is and so mote it be!"

Tear the photo or paper into small pieces and place it in the cauldron.

Take your belongings and place them in the cauldron on top of the paper. The smaller and more flammable the item, the better.

Some witches use clothes for this spell, but a strand of hair or a discarded tissue is just as good – if not better.

When you have everything in the cauldron, set it on fire, and watch it burn. Visualize the spell they put on you dissipating. Its place is filled with dazzling white light and protection.

Flush the ashes down the toilet and wash your hands of any residue.

You are free from the spell!

a spell for
SEPARATION

For this spell you will need:
- Two white candles

Use this spell only if you are still in love with the person who broke up with you, to be able to let them go.

Alternatively, use it with consent from the other person, if you two need to break up for some reason, or if your love is unrequited. Never use it to break a relationship without consent.

The candles represent you and your partner, respectively. The flames represent your passion for each other.

Inscribe your name on one candle, then inscribe the name of the person you want to separate from on the other.

Place the candles next to each other in the middle of your spellcasting place. Light the candles, and say three times:

"Our time together spent, let this relationship now end."

Place the candles a few centimetres apart from each other and let them burn for 13 minutes. Say the spell again and move them even further away.

Let them burn for another 13 minutes.
Repeat the process one last time, so
you have said the spell nine times and
the candles are as far away from each
other as possible.

After you have waited for 13 minutes
for the last time, blow out the candles,
and say:

"So it is and so mote it be."

While you are waiting for 13 minutes,
focus on creating space between you.
The intention should be to let the other
person go, with as little bad feeling
as possible.

a spell to AVOID BECOMING BITTER

For this spell you will need:
- ¾ cups of sugar
- 2 tablespoons of corn syrup
- 2 tablespoons of water
- Grated zest of a lemon

A heartbreak can turn the best people into a shell of themselves. To avoid becoming bitter after a failed relationship, you can use this edible spell to keep yourself in check.

While preparing this lemon candy, pour your intention into it. Repeat:

"Bitter thoughts have no hold on me,

So it is and so mote it be!"

In a saucepan, mix the sugar, corn syrup, and water.

Bring the mixture to a boil and leave on a high heat for about five minutes until it becomes a thick, bubbling liquid.

Switch off the heat and add the lemon zest.

Mix it well, then pour the mixture onto baking paper. Let it cool for a minute. It should be soft but not runny.

Cut it into candy-size pieces with a knife by creating a grid on it. If the lines left by the knife disappear, the mixture is still too hot.

Wait one more minute and try again.

When the mixture has cooled down and becomes solid, break it into pieces.

Put the candy in a container and eat one whenever you have negative thoughts towards your ex or when you notice yourself projecting on people.

The sugar symbolizes your sweet nature that you want to retain.

The lemon is the pain and sadness you went through.

The water and corn syrup symbolize how that experience's influence can never be removed from you, it is now part of who you are. Yet, despite this, you still are a sweet, kind person, who can offer comfort, wisdom, and joy to others, just like this candy.

DIVINATION

The most popular questions fortune tellers receive are all in relation to love. When will I get married? Is he the one? Does he love me? Will he come back?

But divination can do so much more for you. There are far more useful questions you could ask from the tarot, from your wax or tea leaf reading, or the runes. Questions that actually help you find true love.

- What do I need to do to find the one who serves my higher self and purpose?

- What needs to happen before I can get married?

- How can I find a partner who fits my requirements at this moment?

- What kind of energies surround my relationship?

- What kind of intentions does this person have towards me?

- How can I become the best possible partner for my significant other?

Remember:

Questions targeted at actions you could take or things that you should know in order to make better decisions will offer the most valuable information.

CHAPTER
5

HEALING

Trigger warning:
The following chapter contains references
to sexual, physical, and emotional abuse.
Reader discretion is advised.

WHAT
counts as ABUSE
in a RELATION-SHIP?

Many people search longingly for their soulmate or twin flame; however, such yearning can often lead to overlooking the signs of abuse. Oftentimes, abusers ease you into abusive behaviour, and those with narcissistic traits tend to love bomb, which can be misunderstood as their true being. The façade of a soulmate is upheld, and when abuse begins, it is glossed over.

Everyone makes mistakes, but certain patterns transform into abuse. To protect yourself and others, there are many signs to look out for.

the signs of

EMOTIONAL and PSYCHOLOGICAL ABUSE

- Name calling, mocking, shaming, blaming
- Gaslighting and minimizing pain
- Destroying your self-worth and confidence
- Threatening you
- Making baseless accusations

the signs of

SEXUAL and
PHYSICAL ABUSE

- Using force and pressuring you into having sex

- Touching you in a way that makes you uncomfortable

- Hurting you during sex

- Pressuring you into unprotected sex

- Hitting, punching, kicking, pushing, shoving, biting, scratching

- Holding you down, choking, and any physical touch without consent

the signs of
FINANCIAL ABUSE

- Demanding you keep your money in their account

- Controlling and forcing you to justify your expenses

- Taking control of all financial decisions

- Keeping assets in their name and not allowing you to safeguard your own finances

the signs of
COERCIVE CONTROL

- Pressuring you into accepting their rules

- Forcing opinions on you and making you feel abnormal for your own thoughts

- Isolating you from your friends and family

- Forcing you to use shared social media accounts or to share your passwords

- Monitoring and tracking you, including your location

a spell to break a

TRAUMA bond

and create

a TALISMAN

For this spell, you will need:

- A piece of paper and a pen
- A cauldron or a fireproof dish
- A piece of jewellery with a yellow or orange crystal, like citrine, amber, or orange calcite
- A white candle

A **trauma bond** is a phenomenon whereby a victim of abuse develops a bond with the abuser through a cycle of intermittent reward and punishment.

It is not a healthy bond between victims of shared trauma. It keeps many people in unhealthy relationships, because it is so hard to break.

On average, a victim goes back to their abuser 7 times before they can finally break free.

Seek professional help (e.g. Refuge in the UK, or the NCADV in the US) if you feel it is needed. Write down every negative experience you remember and how they made you feel.

You need this list to remind yourself that you are not crazy – as your abuser might suggest. These things did happen to you, and whatever good things they provided you with are not worth going through the bad periods for.

Put this list somewhere safe where you can easily find it, should you contemplate going back.

Light the candle, invoking the cleansing power of fire. On the paper, write the person's name with whom you share a trauma bond. Blot out the name with the pen, willing their influence on you to vanish as their name does under the ink.

Hold the paper above the flame, and let it catch fire. Hold onto it for a few seconds, but don't burn yourself. Place it in the cauldron to burn to ashes.

While you burn the paper, say this three times:

**"Power of fire, I call on thee,
Break this bond and set me free!"**

To make a talisman, hold the jewellery with the crystal to your Third Eye Chakra in the middle of your forehead.

Visualize yourself being surrounded by protective sunshine. It gives you power and joy and fills you with warmth.

Instil this feeling into your crystal, and say three times:

"Crystal of healing, comfort my heart,

Help me keep my head high above,

Restore my self-worth long lost to me,

So it is and so mote it be!"

The spell will help you break the trauma bond. The crystal will remind you of your own worth and give you the courage to stay out of that toxic relationship once and for all.

a major spell to break a

STRONGER TRAUMA bond

For this spell you will need:
- A white or blue candle
- A piece of paper and a white pencil
- A cauldron or fireproof dish
- 13 pinches of salt or earth
- The Full Moon

In case the bond is stronger than you first thought, or if you want to hit it with everything you've got, this is the spell for you.

It will take time and discipline, so only start it if you are ready to finish it. You could use the talisman from the previous spell to give you strength and determination.

You will need to repeat this spell for thirteen days, so fourteen times in total.

Light the candle. It has to be able to burn for at least three hours over the fourteen days. Alternatively, you can use multiple candles, but never change them while the day's ritual is underway.

In your cauldron, add the salt or earth for grounding. Your emotions might be running high while performing this spell, and this will help keep you collected and focused on doing what must be done.

After you have lit the candle, take a small piece of white paper, write your ex's name on it in white so it is difficult to read, then blot it out.

They hold no power over you anymore. Tear the paper and add it into your cauldron.

Let the candle burn for 13 minutes, focusing your intention on breaking the bond and shaking off any power your ex has over you, taking back your power for yourself. Think about everything they have done to you, all the sadness they caused. You could write these things down, doodle your feelings onto paper, or listen to music.

Whatever you do, the focus should be on breaking the bond and reclaiming your power.

When the 13 minutes are done, say three times before blowing out the candle:

**"With this spell I set myself free,
So it is and so mote it be!"**

Keep the candle and the cauldron on your spellcasting space. Repeat this spell a further 13 times.

If at the end of the day's spell the candle looks too small to last for another 13 minutes, let it burn down and replace it with a new one before starting the spell the next day.

On the last day, after tearing up the
name and placing it into the cauldron,
set fire to the pile of paper pieces.
When it is all burned to ashes, mix
it with the salt or earth for a final
cleansing.

If you used earth, go outside and,
facing towards your home, throw the
ashes over your left shoulder, letting
the wind carry them away.

Be mindful of the direction of the wind;
you don't want the ashes to be blown
back towards you.

If you used salt, empty the cauldron's contents into the toilet, close the lid, and flush it away. Salt can make earth infertile; you shouldn't dispose of it outside.

Wash your hands, getting rid of any residue the ashes might have left on them.

Let the candle burn down and throw whatever is left of it in the bin. You are now free from the trauma bond.

Additional tips

1. Before spellcasting, understand how and why the spell works.

2. Casting spells that are successful for you is really a voyage of self-discovery.

3. You will only realize what works for you after conducting numerous spells.

4. Never give up.

If on your first attempt, your spell did not produce the intended effect, try again, perhaps with different objects on your altar and using different techniques, changing the way you cast the spell rather than repeating the same one.

CONCLUSION

never cast spells to cause harm to others, because the harm will come back on you three times as badly.

always remember to keep an eye on candles while they are burning and never leave them unguarded.

remember to follow the guidelines and always work for the good of all concerned. Do not be afraid to experiment with all the different materials that are available to you and remember to be patient and not expect immediate results. As with everything, spellcasting takes practice, practice, and more practice! Good luck!